First World War
and Army of Occupation
War Diary
France, Belgium and Germany

59 DIVISION
177 Infantry Brigade
Leicestershire Regiment
2/5th Battalion
1 February 1917 - 31 January 1918

WO95/3022/6

The Naval & Military Press Ltd
www.nmarchive.com
Published in association with The National Archives

Published by

The Naval & Military Press Ltd

Unit 10 Ridgewood Industrial Park,

Uckfield, East Sussex,

TN22 5QE England

Tel: +44 (0) 1825 749494

www.naval-military-press.com

www.nmarchive.com

This diary has been reprinted in facsimile from the original. Any imperfections are inevitably reproduced and the quality may fall short of modern type and cartographic standards.

© **Crown Copyright**
Images reproduced by permission of The National Archives, London, England, 2015.

Contents

Document type	Place/Title	Date From	Date To
Heading	WO95/3022/6 1917 Feb-1918 Jan 2/5 Battalion Leicestershire Regiment		
Heading	2/5th Bn Leicesters Feb 1917-Jan 1918 And 1916 Jan-Feb		
War Diary	Fovant	01/02/1917	24/02/1917
War Diary	Havre	25/02/1917	25/02/1917
War Diary	Saleux	26/02/1917	26/02/1917
War Diary	Petit St Jean	27/02/1917	01/03/1917
War Diary	Fouencamps	02/03/1917	02/03/1917
War Diary	Morcourt	04/03/1917	08/03/1917
War Diary	Bois Triangulaire	09/03/1917	12/03/1917
War Diary	P C Nancy	13/03/1917	20/03/1917
War Diary	Foucaucourt	26/03/1917	26/03/1917
War Diary	Le Mesnil	27/03/1917	27/03/1917
War Diary	Hancourt	27/03/1917	30/03/1917
War Diary	Roisel	31/03/1917	31/03/1917
War Diary	Hesbecourt	01/04/1917	12/04/1917
War Diary	Hervilly	13/04/1917	15/04/1917
War Diary	Brosse Woods	16/04/1917	17/04/1917
War Diary	Hervilly	18/04/1917	19/04/1917
War Diary	Hancourt	20/04/1917	28/04/1917
War Diary	Leverguier	29/04/1917	15/05/1917
War Diary	Bois Bias	15/05/1917	25/05/1917
War Diary	Equancourt	26/05/1917	27/05/1917
War Diary	Villers Plouich	28/05/1917	07/06/1917
War Diary	Dessart Wood	08/06/1917	17/06/1917
War Diary	Villers Plouich	18/06/1917	22/06/1917
War Diary	Equancourt	23/06/1917	01/07/1917
War Diary	Metz-En-Couture	02/07/1917	05/07/1917
War Diary	Bilhem	06/07/1917	10/07/1917
War Diary	Equancourt	10/07/1917	10/07/1917
War Diary	Barastre	11/07/1917	22/08/1917
War Diary	Senlis (v.10.d)	23/08/1917	31/08/1917
War Diary	In The Train	01/09/1917	01/09/1917
War Diary	Winnezeele	02/09/1917	20/09/1917
War Diary	Esk Camp	21/09/1917	22/09/1917
War Diary	St Jean	23/09/1917	24/09/1917
War Diary	Bank Farm	25/09/1917	25/09/1917
War Diary	Elmtree Corner	26/09/1917	26/09/1917
War Diary	Hill 27	27/09/1917	29/09/1917
War Diary	Old German Front Line	30/09/1917	30/09/1917
War Diary	Vlamertinge	01/10/1917	01/10/1917
War Diary	Thiennes	02/10/1917	06/10/1917
War Diary	Beaumetz-Lez-Aire	07/10/1917	10/10/1917
War Diary	Camblain Chatelain	11/10/1917	11/10/1917
War Diary	Houdain	12/10/1917	12/10/1917
War Diary	Gouy-Servins	13/10/1917	13/10/1917
War Diary	Tottenham Camp	13/10/1917	13/10/1917
War Diary	Old Brewery	14/10/1917	17/10/1917
War Diary	Piano Dug Out	18/10/1917	21/10/1917

War Diary	Alberta Camp	22/10/1917	28/10/1917
War Diary	Lievin	29/10/1917	13/11/1917
War Diary	Petit Servins	14/11/1917	17/11/1917
War Diary	Habarcq	18/11/1917	19/11/1917
War Diary	Bailleulval	20/11/1917	21/11/1917
War Diary	Henham Camp South	22/11/1917	23/11/1917
War Diary	Dessart Wood	24/11/1917	27/11/1917
War Diary	Trescauclt	28/11/1917	28/11/1917
War Diary	Flesquires	29/11/1917	02/12/1917
War Diary	Cantaing Mill	03/12/1917	04/12/1917
War Diary	Flesquires Church	05/12/1917	05/12/1917
War Diary	Old Bde HQ Flesquires	06/12/1917	09/12/1917
War Diary	Trescauclt	10/12/1917	10/12/1917
War Diary	Lechelle	11/12/1917	14/12/1917
War Diary	Trescauclt	15/12/1917	17/12/1917
War Diary	Hindenburg Support	18/12/1917	22/12/1917
War Diary	Butlers Cross	23/12/1917	23/12/1917
War Diary	Rocquigny	24/12/1917	25/12/1917
War Diary	Penin	26/12/1917	30/01/1918
War Diary	Lignereuil	31/01/1918	31/01/1918

WO/95/3022/6

1917 Feb - 1918 Jan

2/5 Battalion Leicestershire Regiment.

59TH DIVISION
177TH INFY BDE

2-5TH BN LEICESTERS.
FEB 1917 – JAN 1918.

AND
1916 JAN - & FEB

DISBANDED

SECRET

122/39 February 1917

Army Form C. 2118.

WAR DIARY
or
INTELLIGENCE SUMMARY.

(Erase heading not required.)

2/5 S. Staffs. Regt.

Instructions regarding War Diaries and Intelligence Summaries are contained in F.S. Regs., Part II. and the Staff Manual respectively. Title pages will be prepared in manuscript.

Hour, Date, Place	Summary of Events and Information	Remarks and references to Appendices
16.18 February FOVANT	In Camp (huts) final embarkation for movement.	Not
24 "	Entrained at DINTON for SOUTHAMPTON — en route for B.E.F. Crossed to HAVRE.	
25 " HAVRE	5 hours at GARE de MARCHANDISES.	
26 " ST LE OY	Detrained and marched to PETIT ST JEAN	
27.28 " PETIT ST JEAN	In billets.	

W.P. Robs. Capt & M/or
Commanding 2/5 S. Staffords Reg.

SECRET 177/59

Army Form C. 2118.

2/5 Leicestershire Regt.

Vol II

WAR DIARY
INTELLIGENCE SUMMARY

March 1917

(Erase heading not required.)

Hour, Date, Place	Summary of Events and Information	Remarks and references to Appendices
1st March, 1917. PETIT-ST-JEAN.	Marched to FOUENCAMPS. Occupied billets.	
2nd FOUENCAMPS.	Marched to CAMP 59, near MORCOURT. Occupied huttments.	
4th MORCOURT	Sent 1 Officer per Company - 1 N.C.O & 2 men per platoon to trenches at BOIS TRIANGULAIRE to be attached to Battalion in Reserve, 1/4 E/York	
8th MORCOURT	Marched to BOIS TRIANGULAIRE & took over trenches as Battalion in Brigade Reserve. 4 Coys in Support, 4 & 5 trenches in front line	
9th to 12th BOIS TRIANGULAIRE.	In Brigade Reserve.	

WAR DIARY or INTELLIGENCE SUMMARY

Army Form C. 2118.

(Erase heading not required.)

Instructions regarding War Diaries and Intelligence Summaries are contained in F.S. Regs., Part II. and the Staff Manual respectively. Title pages will be prepared in manuscript.

Hour, Date, Place	Summary of Events and Information	Remarks and references to Appendices
12th March. BOIS TRIANGULAIRE	Relieves 5th Leinster Regt in front line — see left instruction in Brigade Orders. 4th Leicestershire on right, 6th Leicester Regt on 1st Division on our left. H.Q. P.C. NANCY. A & C Coys in front line. B Coy in support. D Coy in reserve.	
13th March. P.C. NANCY.		
14th " P.C. NANCY.	B Coy relieves C Coy in front line — nights 14th/15th. B Coy relieves A Coy in front line — nights 15th/16th.	
15th " "		
16th " "	Normal.	
17th " "		
18th " "	Reports receive that enemy has retired — patrols pushed forward in Northern	
19th " "	advanced and occupies enemy trenches on far side ARGUS Trench, where line was consolidated — patrols pushed forward to SOMME R. and reports no enemy in sight. Further Consolidation of position — ARGUS TRENCH — patrols crossed SOMME R. and reported no enemy in sight.	
20th " "	1st Division on our left, moved forward to position in ERFURT TRENCH & to south east BIAZ R. SOMME. Relieved by 5th Sherwood Foresters — marches to Divisional rest at FOUCAUCOURT (CANTONNEMENT DES POMMIERS)	
26th " FOUCAUCOURT	Marches to LE MESNIL	
27th " LE MESNIL	Marches to HANCOURT, which was occupied + held by 18th Bengal Lancers, 4.5.E.	
27th–29th HANCOURT	Div. Cyclists & later 2/5th Sherwood Foresters. Working parties nightly to make line of Caucasian posts east of NOBESCOURT FARM.	
30th HANCOURT		
31st Hancourt ROISEL	Marches to ROISEL	
1 p.m.	Artillery commences intense bombardment on HERVILLY and HESBECOURT. C Company patrol reported HERVILLY clear. One platoon of C. Co. entered HERVILLY.	
1.45 p.m.	Drove out enemy patrol + capturing one wounded prisoner. Outpost pushed out to east end of HERVILLY WOOD.	
2.30 p.m.	Attack launched on HESBECOURT. A Company on left, D Company on right	

Army Form C. 2118.

WAR DIARY
or
INTELLIGENCE SUMMARY.
(Erase heading not required.)

Instructions regarding War Diaries and Intelligence Summaries are contained in F.S. Regs., Part II. and the Staff Manual respectively. Title pages will be prepared in manuscript.

Hour, Date, Place	Summary of Events and Information	Remarks and references to Appendices
2.25 p.m.	Attack held up for 20 minutes by machine guns. Advance continued. Enemy seen to be retiring from HESBECOURT.	
3.0 p.m.	HESBECOURT occupied. A covering line 1000 yards east of the Village taken up. The village heavily shelled. Casualties incurred. Companies reorganised	
4.15 p.m.	C attack HILL 140. B. Company as reserve moved up into HESBECOURT. Patrols up to HILL 140 clear. A. & D. Companies advanced & occupied HILL 140. Battalion Headquarters moved to HESBECOURT.	
5.0 p.m. onwards.	Position from the neighbourhood of L 26.A.9.1. to L 80.54 consolidated. C. Company thrown out as outpost line in front of this line. Casualties, Major R.P. Shea wounded. One man killed, 18 wounded, 5 missing.	

Approved LtCol
2/5 Leicestershire Regt.

WAR DIARY or INTELLIGENCE SUMMARY

Army Form C. 2118.

2/5 Leicestershire Regt.   April, 1917

Hour, Date, Place	Summary of Events and Information	Remarks and references to Appendices
1st April 1917. HESBECOURT	Line of Cruciform posts begun at L.26.A.22, L.20.A.41, L.14.C.53, L.14.A.47, L.7.C.95, L.7.A.51. On right junction obtained with 2/6th Sherwood Foresters.	OK 7
2nd 10 p.m. HESBECOURT	TEMPLEUX occupied by 1 pot. Brigade. 1 gun sent to HESBECOURT. Cruciform posts and HESBECOURT shelled intermittently during day. Post reoccupied.	OK 7
7.30 p.m. to 8.30 p.m.	CARPEZA COPSE throughout day.	OK 7
8.30 p.m.	Artillery preparation. B. & C. Companies in support to 4th Leicesters in attack on FERVAQUE FARM. Attack held up, hardly through wire and machine gun, partly.	OK 7
3rd HESBECOURT 8.30 p.m. 9.15 p.m.	Through failure of 178th Brigade to take LE VERGUIER. B & C Companies took over front line during evening. Artillery preparation. 2/4th Lincolns attacked FERVAQUE FARM, but failed owing to inability to cross wire.	OK 7
4th HESBECOURT to 6.30 p.m.	2/5 Lincs maintained former line after failure of attack. 3/4 Leicesters relieved C. during evening. Posts established in TEMPLEUX.	OK 7
5th HESBECOURT 7.0 a.m.	48th Division on left carried out successful attack on RONSSY, BASSE - BOUL-OGNE & LEMPIRE. Line held, L.15.A.88 to TEMPLEUX.	OK 7
6th HESBECOURT	A Company relieved B. on night 7 Draw 30 on left. New Cruciform posts begun. Cruciform posts shelled. Little shelling. C in kids. B.A. out in support during early morning. Orderly patrolled but not occupied.	OK 7
7th HESBECOURT 10 a.m.	Cruciform posts occupied at L.15.A.37 - L.9.C.28 - L.9.B.central. C.C. in support B.E in kids. 3 new posts dug during night at L.15.B.35 - L.7.D.34 - L.9.D.82.	OK 7

Army Form C. 2118.

WAR DIARY
or
INTELLIGENCE SUMMARY.
(Erase heading not required.)

Instructions regarding War Diaries and Intelligence Summaries are contained in F.S. Regs., Part II. and the Staff Manual respectively. Title pages will be prepared in manuscript.

Hour, Date, Place	Summary of Events and Information	Remarks and references to Appendices
8th April 1917 NESSECOURT	h.h. in new trenches posts to gr. R.D. & forward observation posts N side D 6d.	O.K.J.
9" NESSECOURT 7 a.m.	prepared to advance in support but owing to rebury, status sent out, but...	O.K.J.
	Pkd. of D Coy. in farm & bill... Farm [illegible] occupied 2/L.E. Dur. right.	
5.25p	FERVACQUE FARM occupied by patrol of D.C. Enemy front line trenches found to right unoccupied. Junction made with 178 Brigade & to approach junction made with 2/5 Lancers.	
9 p.	Battalion relieved by 2/4 Lancashire & returned to NESSECOURT.	
10 " NESSECOURT 3.30a	Relief complete.	O.K.J.
11"	2/5 D. Company went to HERVILLY.	O.K.J.
	A party worked at HARBLET.	
	Wellington's built on new line commenced.	
12" NESSECOURT	Headquarters & 2 Companies to HAMELET.	O.K.J.
	Headquarters moved to HERVILLY.	
13" HERVILLY	Wiring parties continued.	
	Working parties continued.	O.K.J.
	Reconnaissance of VILLERET & L.17.18.	O.K.J.
14"	—	O.K.J.
15" HERVILLY 9.30 p.	Attack of VILLERET & high ground to south of it. B.C. on the right, C.C. on left. A.C. giving support & D.C. reserve. Headquarters moved to BROSSE WOODS. Objectives gained. Both Coys. carried rifle-fits with the bayonet. B. & C. Companies	D.6.J.
11.30 p.	secured VILLERET with shouts & bayonets.	
16" BROSSE WOODS	Posts established at L.18.A.26, L.17.B.94, L.17.D.66, L.17.B.68 & L.17.D.45; consolidated gradually.	O.K.J.
4.6 a.m.	Heavy enemy barrage fired, retaliation by own guns. Casualties - 6 killed & 20 % wounds, 17 wounded, 1 missing	
10.0 p.	Relief commenced by 2/4 Lancashire.	
1.30 a.	Relief complete A & D Companies to TEMPLEUX; B.C. & H.Q. to HERVILLY. 2/L.F. B & C & 2/L.F. North. posts to A & D Companies	O.K.J.

WAR DIARY
or
INTELLIGENCE SUMMARY.
(Erase heading not required.)

Army Form C. 2118.

Hour, Date, Place		Summary of Events and Information	Remarks and references to Appendices
18th	HERVILLY	6 p.m. — Battalion moved into support of 7/4th Lincolns in their attack on VILLERET. Attack partially successful. Suffolk not called on	O.H.3
19th	HERVILLY	5 a.m. A & D Companies withdrawn from support of A. HESSECOURT, B.C. & H.Q. to HERVILLY	O.H.3
		11 p.m. Battalion relieved by 2/5 Sherwood Foresters, & proceeded into Divisional Reserve at HANCOURT.	O.H.3
20th	HANCOURT	Cleaning up & working parties.	O.H.3
21st	HANCOURT	Cleaning up & working parties	O.H.3
22nd	HANCOURT	Inspection by Major General Romer. 91st Battalion in mass without transport.	O.H.3
23rd	HANCOURT	Specialist Training & Working Parties.	O.H.3
24th	HANCOURT	Specialist Training & Working Parties	O.H.3
25th	HANCOURT	Working Parties	O.H.3
26th	HANCOURT	Specialist Training & Working Parties. Relieving front line reconnoitred by C.O., Adjt, C.O.'s Companies, I.O. & S.O.	O.H.3
		6.15 p.m. "B" Company caught fire & totally destroyed. Some equipment lost but no men injured	
27th	HANCOURT	Working parties. Relief postponed.	O.H.3
28th	HANCOURT	HANCOURT bombarded during the night. Casualties 2nd Battalion nil. 2/6 South Staffords and Regt in front line. ASCENSION FARM	O.H.3
		to GRAND PRIEL FARM. B.C. D + 2 Platoons of A Coy in front line, 7 local supports. Battalion H.Q. established in quarry at L.28.A.5.4. noon	
29th	LE VERGIER	1.18 a.m. LE VERGIER Relief complete.	O.H.3
		Casualty one man killed during morning. Front line 1 post at map refs L.30.E.80 - G.25.D.34 - L.30.C.106 - L.30.A.54 - L.24.C.51, L.24.C.88 - L.24.A.20. Connects with 2/5 Lincolns at G.31.B.54 & 2/5 Sherwood Foresters at L.18.C.37	
		9.30 p.m. Took over 2/5 Sherwood Foresters line as far as L.17.D.71, two platoons 7 A Coy taking over the additional line. Two platoons of A.C. withdrawn from B & D Companies	

O.M.Wood Lt Col Commanding 1/5 Suffolk Regt

Army Form C. 2118.

WAR DIARY
or
INTELLIGENCE SUMMARY.
(Erase heading not required.)

Instructions regarding War Diaries and Intelligence Summaries are contained in F.S. Regs., Part II. and the Staff Manual respectively. Title pages will be prepared in manuscript.

Hour, Date, Place	Summary of Events and Information	Remarks and references to Appendices
30th LE VERGIER	One man killed during night. Advanced posts began taking the night at G.25.D.34 — G.25.B.39 — L.24.A.72 L.24.A.18. Wing Dangers. Reinforcement of 7 other ranks arrived.	O.K.7.

CMMWard Lt. Col.
Comd. 2/5

ORIGINAL

SECRET

MAY 1917

Army Form C. 2118.

2/5 Leicestershire Regiment

WAR DIARY
or
INTELLIGENCE SUMMARY.
(Erase heading not required.)

Instructions regarding War Diaries and Intelligence Summaries are contained in F.S. Regs., Part II. and the Staff Manual respectively. Title pages will be prepared in manuscript.

Hour, Date, Place		Summary of Events and Information	Remarks and references to Appendices
MAY 1917			
1st LE VERGUIER		Front line posts held. New posts established at G.25.D.17, 43.C.A.79, G.25.B.39, L.24.A.73 & 38. Major T.C.P. Beasley & 2/Lt. S.G.N. Steele reported for duty from Base. Battalion relieved by 2/4 Leicestershire & withdrew into 2/5 Bde in L.27.B. Headquarters.	O.A.7.
2nd			O.A.3.
3rd	1.20 am	Relief complete. Strength 8 & Battalion 34 officers 819 other ranks. Trench strength 26 officers 669. Held Support line in Main Line of Resistance under Royal Engineers	O.A.3.
4th		Working parties as before	O.A.3.
5th		Working parties as before	O.A.3.
	10.10 pm	2/5 Leicesters 6 night relief of Regiment attacked by a stout patrol Battalion 2nd Lt. C. & D. Companies going to 2/5 Lincoln Headquarters as Bivouac.	O.A.3.
6th	4.6 am	Battalion normal. C. & D. Companies returned. Working parties & main line of resistance	O.A.3.
7th		2/Lt. R.A. Searle & 2/Lt. F.C. Robinson joined for duty from Base	O.A.3.
8th		3/4 Leicestershire relieved us. B and D Companies to Headquarters not changed.	O.A.3.
	12.25 am	Relief complete. C.D. & A Companies in the ? B.C. in support in 6 German	O.A.3.
9th		trenches. Quiet.	O.A.3.
10th	2.0 am	2/Lt FEATHERSTON's train encountered strong enemy piquet at G.20.A.39.	O.A.3.
		One man killed. Enterprise enemy actively until dawn. Gaps opened, but short of a continuous found line. Enborsing most of the routes forward tried. Battalion relieved by 2/4 Leicesters & withdrew to 2/5 German line	O.A.3.
11th			O.A.3.
12th	1.5 am	Relief complete. Working parties on main line of resistance Working parties as before	O.A.3.
13th		Working parties as before	O.A.3.
14th			O.A.3.
15th		The Brigade relieved by Sixmoleana Cavalry Brigade. The Battalion relieved by 2nd Dragoons. Moved and marched back to a training camp at P.16 central, between Bouvincourt & Vraignes	O.A.3.

(73989) W.4141—463. 400,000. 9/14. H.& J.Ltd. Forms/C. 2118/10.

SECRET Page 2. Army Form C. 2118.

2/5 Leicestershire Regt.

WAR DIARY
or
INTELLIGENCE SUMMARY.
(Erase heading not required.)

Hour, Date, Place	Summary of Events and Information	Remarks and references to Appendices
May 1917 BOIS BIAS 15th 12.15 p.m. (continued)	Relief complete. Battalion cleaning up. A body accidentally exploded wounding six of the guard.	O.K.3
16th —	No further incident.	O.K.3
17th —	Individual training of B+D Companies commenced. Platoon training of A+C.	O.K.3
18th —	Training continued.	O.K.3
19th —	Training continued.	O.K.3
20th —	Brigade Church Parade. At the close of the service, Major General Romer presented Distinguished Conduct Crosses to No. 240621 Private G.H. Farrar, C.C. for good work at VILLERET, and No. 241249 Lance Corporal W Drury and 241983 Private J Godber 1 D. Co. for good work at FERVAQUE FARM.	O.K.3
21st —	Training continued.	O.K.3
22nd —	Wet. No training possible.	O.K.3
23rd —	Brigade parade for inspection of rifles. The Battalion afterwards inspected by the Brigadier General Commanding. Training continued. No. 240647 Cpt. P. Francis of "D" Co. awarded the D.C.M. for gallantry at FERVAQUE FARM on 9.4.1917.	O.K.3
24th —	Training continued. A+C Companies commenced Individual Training. B+D Platoon training.	O.K.3
25th —	The Battalion moved by march route to EQUANCOURT, by way of CARTIGNY, TINCOURT, TEMPLEUX-LE-FOSSE, AIZECOURT-LE-BAS, & NURLU. 2 coys at V.10.B.9.3. A very hot day. Brigade came under 42nd Division.	O.K.3
26th EQUANCOURT	Commanding Officer and Coy Commanders went to reconnoitre line to be taken over from 6th Lancashire Fusiliers.	O.K.3
27th EQUANCOURT	Brigade Church Parade. Brigade took over the line held by 125th Infantry Brigade from R.7939 to Q.12C73. The Battalion took over the sub-sector of this line with A & D Companies in front line & C.C. in support. Headquarters in a sunken road at Q.18B.98. Quartermaster's Store and Transport at	O.K.3

W.W.Wood Lt Col
2/5 Leicestershire Regt

SECRET

Army Form C. 2118.

Instructions regarding War Diaries and Intelligence Summaries are contained in F.S. Regs., Part II and the Staff Manual respectively. Title pages will be prepared in manuscript.

2/5 Leicestershire Regt.

WAR DIARY
or
INTELLIGENCE SUMMARY.
(Erase heading not required.)

Hour, Date, Place	Summary of Events and Information	Remarks and references to Appendices
May 1917		
28th. VILLERS PLOUICH 1.30pm	Relief completed. Wiring by night, dug also a communication trench to improved advanced posts.	O.H.7.
29th	On night of improved. B Company relieved by C. Co. in centre. Work continued.	O.H.7.
30th	Left Company pushed forward men of 2/5 Lincolns as far as Q.12.D.78. A Coy. shortly after left supported near trenches Right Coy.(D.)	O.H.7. O.H.7.
31st	Relief in afternoon as no more killed. New line of posts commenced about 400 yds in advance of existing front system.	O.H.7.

J.D.W. Wood Lt Col
2/5 Leicestershire Regt

SECRET

ORIGINAL SECRET

Army Form C. 2118.

2/5 Leicestershire Regt.

WAR DIARY
INTELLIGENCE SUMMARY.
(Erase heading not required.)

Instructions regarding War Diaries and Intelligence Summaries are contained in F.S. Regs., Part II. and the Staff Manual respectively. Title pages will be prepared in manuscript.

Hour, Date, Place	Summary of Events and Information	Remarks and references to Appendices
JUNE, 1917		
1st VILLERS PLOUICH	Quiet throughout day. Strength, 35 officers & 782 O.R. Arrivals strength, 24 off. 649 O.R. A Coy of advanced posts began at R7 > 1364. (Ashby Post), R7R27 (roughly) R7A central (Carlisle Post). Heavy enemy fire on the night throughout most of the night. Casualties, one private other ranks 7 wounded.	O.H.7
p.m.	B Company relieved D in front line.	
2nd	Enemy shelled night of main line.	O.H.7
3.0 a.m.	Work continued. C. Company relieves A on our right.	O.H.7
p.m.	Heavy enemy bombardment & barrage on division on our right. All quiet	O.H.7
4th 2.0 a.m.	on our sector. Captain Paragraph wounded.	O.H.7
p.m.	Work continued. Communication trench got through to Ashby Post.	
5th	Advance parties of relieving unit arrived. Work continued. Communication	O.H.7
	trench to Carlisle Post got through.	
6th p.m.	Relieved by 2/4 Leicestershire Regt.	O.H.7
7th 12.5 a.m.	Relief complete. Battalion moved to Brigade Reserve at W1B17.	O.H.7
	Working parties. First draft of 13 men.	O.H.7
8th DESSART WOOD 1.45 a.m.	Gas alarm. Alarm cancelled after half an hour.	O.H.7
9th	Working parties.	O.H.7
	Working parties. Sergt Major class for young N.C.O. commenced.	O.H.7
10th	Working parties. Church Parade in the shade in DESSART WOOD. D.C.M.	O.H.7
	presented to No. 240647, Cpl. P. Francis of "D" Co. by Major General Romer	
11th	Working parties.	O.H.7
12th	Working parties.	O.H.7
13th	Working parties.	O.H.7
14th	Working parties.	O.H.7
15th	Working parties.	O.H.7
	No. 242198 Private C.J. Redwood of "B" Co. awarded Military Medal for gallantry	O.H.7
	at post on night of our raid on 4.6.1917.	

W.K.Ward Lt Col

SECRET   Army Form C. 2118.

Instructions regarding War Diaries and Intelligence
Summaries are contained in F.S. Regs., Part II
and the Staff Manual respectively. Title pages
will be prepared in manuscript.

WAR DIARY
or
INTELLIGENCE SUMMARY.
(Erase heading not required.)

2/5 Leicestershire Regt.

Hour, Date, Place	Summary of Events and Information	Remarks and references to Appendices
15th (cont.d) DESSART WOOD	No. 241839 Private L. B. Page of "B" Company awarded commendation card for gallantry on 1.6.1917. Working parties. Advance post wires front line.	O.A.7
16th DESSART WOOD		O.A.7
17th —	Relieved 2/4th Leicestershire Regt. in front line. Battalion H.Q. at Q15 B 9.8. Lines of posts. Slight shelling. No resistance on front. "B" & "C" Coys. front line. "A" Coy in support. "D" Coy. at Bn. HQ. Left front line. D. in night. "B" Coy on support & "A" Coy. at Bn. HQ. R.E. for cable laying 2 night laying.	O.A.7
18th VILLERS PLOUICH 2 a.m.	Relief complete. Heavy rain. Trenches very wet. At work on draining and latching of front line posts. 2/Lt A. B. Bedford - 2/Lt N.R Bilson reported for duty.	O.A.7
19th — " —	Work continued on improvement of posts. Weather still very wet. Line now holds with 9 posts.	O.A.7
20th — " —	Drawings of trenches & much improved. Work on front line continued. Capt W.E. Porter wounded by sniper. Advance party of 2/1 S.F. arrived.	O.A.7
21st — " —	Relieved by 3 Companies of 2/6 Sherwood Foresters. "A" Company left Latrine on Transit Line to continue cable laying.	O.A.7
22nd — " — 2.0 a.m.	Relief complete. The Battalion moved into Divisional Reserve into camp at V16.13.53. Cleaning up all day.	O.A.7
23rd EQUANCOURT 3.30 p.m.	Cleaning up. Battalion Commanding Officers Inspection. Brigade Parade for total Distribution by Major General G. F. Rowan. 2/Lt G.M. Laird received Military Cross for gallantry near VILLERS PLOUICH on 1 June. L/Cpl. Ridings received Military Medal.	O.A.7
24th — " —	Brigade Parade service. Jun platoons "A" Coy rejoined on relief.	O.A.7
25th — " —	Individual Training + Company Attack Training. Commandg. C. Co. fire course on 30x range.	O.A.7
26th — " —	Training continued. "B" Company on range.	O.A.7

JM Wood Lieut

Army Form C. 2118.

2/5 Leicestershire Regt.

WAR DIARY
or
INTELLIGENCE SUMMARY.
(Erase heading not required.)

Hour, Date, Place	Summary of Events and Information	Remarks and references to Appendices
27th EQUANCOURT	Training continued. D.C. on range. Remainder of A.C. rejoined from detachment.	O.H.7.
28th —	Training continued. A.Co. on range. Brigade sports in afternoon.	O.H.7.
29th —	Training continued. Brigade Sports in afternoon. The Battalion beaten in championship by one point by 2/5 Lincolns.	O.H.7.
30th —	Training continued. Advance party marched to METZ-EN-COUTURE. Brigade rifle meeting. The Battalion won all rifle events, & in all five prizes out of eight.	O.H.7.

QMcgWood Lieut Col
2/5th Leicestershire Regt.

Original   Reference Map/C. 57c.

SECRET.   Army Form C. 2118.

Instructions regarding War Diaries and Intelligence
Summaries are contained in F.S. Regs., Part II.   2/5th The Leicestershire Regt
and the Staff Manual respectively. Title pages
will be prepared in manuscript.

WAR DIARY
or
INTELLIGENCE SUMMARY.
(Erase heading not required.)

JULY 1917

Hour, Date, Place		Summary of Events and Information	Remarks and references to Appendices
JULY 1917			
1st EQUANCOURT		177th Infantry Brigade relieved 178th Infantry Brigade in BILHEM sector.	O.K.3.
		2/5th North Staffordshire Regt. as support Battalion.	O.K.3.
	8.20pm	Battalion refused at METZ-EN-COUTURE. Headquarters at Q.19.D.9.9. Companies occupied	
		Batterson line trenches from Q.14.C.17 to Q.21.C.13.	
		Relief completed.	
2nd METZ-EN-COUTURE		Working parties under R.E. Officer.	O.K.3.
3rd	1.30am	Gas alarm, cancelled after 30 minutes.	O.K.3.
		Working parties.	
4th	12.15am	Gas alarm, cancelled after 35 minutes.	O.K.3.
		Working parties.	
5th		Advance parties visited line. 1st Lincolnshire Regt arrangements made for relief of the	O.K.3.
		Brigade front. Part of relief carried out in daylight by communication	
		trenches. A & B Companies in front line, C.G in support, D in reserve.	
		Battalion Headquarters & Hllrs formed at Q.10.D.4.8.	
	11.50pm	3rd Lincolnshire Company killed by shell fire during relief.	
		Relief completed.	
		Troops on left picked up & trench TRESCAULT-RIBECOURT road and a post	O.K.3.
6th BILHEM		gained at Q.5.A.8.2.	
7th		Bombard shelling enemy light part of Q.5.A.8.2 occupied by A.C.	O.K.3.
8th	—	Work continued at night & relieving week around.	O.K.3.
9th	—	Aroma party & relieving work around. One man of "B" Co. many killers.	O.K.3.
10th	1.30am	Further shelling in morning.	O.I.5
		Battalion relieved by 2/5th Lindse Regiment. Two 2 Companies in the line	O.K.3.
		During evening party the line.	
		Relief completed. Companies moved to HAVRINCOURT WOOD thence by	
		Decauville to FINS, & thence marched to former camp at EQUANCOURT	
		at VIGD.	O.W.WOAK A.C.A

Original

SECRET JULY 1917

Army Form C. 2118.

Instructions regarding War Diaries and Intelligence Summaries are contained in F.S. Regs., Part II. and the Staff Manual respectively. Title pages will be prepared in manuscript.

WAR DIARY
or
INTELLIGENCE SUMMARY.
(Erase heading not required.)

2/5th 13th The Leicestershire Regt.

Hour, Date, Place		Summary of Events and Information	Remarks and references to Appendices
July 1917			
10th EQUANCOURT	12 noon	Battalion moved with Bde to Brigade camp at O.16.D., arriving at 3.25 p.m.	O.N.T.
11th BARASTRE		The Division came under IV Corps of 3rd Army. Rest & cleaning up.	O.K.T.
12th —	—	Training commenced.	O.K.T.
13th —	—	Training continued. Firing on range commenced.	O.K.T.
14th —	—	Training continued.	O.K.T.
15th —	—	Brigade Chief Parade. Battalion attack in the open.	O.K.T.
16th —	—	Training continued.	O.K.T.
17th —	—	Training continued.	O.K.T.
18th —	—	Training continued.	O.K.T.
19th —	—	The Battalion won jumping competition & was three for watercarts.	O.K.T.
20th —	—	Training continued. Number events of Divisional Sports afternoon.	O.N.T.
21st —	—	Training continued. Divisional Sports in afternoon. The Battalion won Relay Race & Officers' Race, was 2nd in 100 yds, & in semi-final of Tug of War.	O.K.T.
22nd —	—	Church Parade.	O.K.T.
23rd —	—	Training continued. A & C Companies fired on range at N&D noon. LIGNY – THILLOY.	O.K.T.
24th —	—	Training continued.	O.K.T.
25th —	—	Training continued. Divisional tactical training at BARASTRE.	O.K.T.
26th —	—	Training continued.	O.K.T.
27th —	—	Divisional tactical scheme. Attack on Am Support from SOMME to LE TRANSLOY – SAILLY SAILLISEL Road, 3rd Brigade as base had had for U.1.B.63 & N.36.D.42 Same Road U.1.B.84.2 & Same objective U.2.A.17.6 031/A.21. Battn objective 031/B/10	
			(signed) W Wm L† Col

Original

July 1917

SECRET

Army Form C. 2118.

Instructions regarding War Diaries and Intelligence Summaries are contained in F.S. Regs., Part II and the Staff Manual respectively. Title pages will be prepared in manuscript.

WAR DIARY
or
INTELLIGENCE SUMMARY.
(Erase heading not required.)

2/5th B. The Leicestershire Regt.

Hour, Date, Place July, 1917	Summary of Events and Information	Remarks and references to Appendices
27th (continued) 13 ARRASTRE	to 031 A 99. 178th Brigade on right & 177th Brigade on left. 2/4th Leicesters supported in 2/5th Leicesters & 2/5th Leicestershire	O.R.Y.
	Light railway front line. 2/4th Leicesters pushed in support. 2/5th Leicestershire relieved the Brigade constants after repairing the line & pushing	
	the 178th Brigade who were out down & consolidated the ground objective	
28th	Enemy reported to 2/177th Brigade Afternoon 2/4th & 2/5th Leicestershire	O.R.Y.
	relieved 2/4th & 2/5th Leicesters in front line Brigade	
29th	Colonel Radcliffe D.S.O. of 17th other ranks arrived	O.R.Y.
30th	Trusting continued. Battalion returned to its open Dugs of 17 other ranks	O.R.Y.
31st	continued	
	Training continues.	

(73989) W4141—463. 400,000. 9/14. H.&J.Ltd. Forms/C. 2118/10.

ORIGINAL

SECRET
Army Form C. 2118.

2/5 Leicestershire Regt

WAR DIARY
INTELLIGENCE SUMMARY
(Erase heading not required.)

AUGUST 1917

Instructions regarding War Diaries and Intelligence Summaries are contained in F.S. Regs., Part II. and the Staff Manual respectively. Title pages will be prepared in manuscript.

Place	Date	Hour	Summary of Events and Information	Remarks and references to Appendices
	1917. August			France. 57/C. 57 C.NW
BARASTRE (6.16.d)	1		Training continued. Individual training	O.H.7.
	2		Training continued. Individual training	O.H.7.
	3		Training continued. Individual training	O.H.7.
	4		2.30p Tactical Exercise for Officers of the Division with Platoon Nucleus, (Infantry & Battalion Runners)	O.H.7.
	4		Training continued. Royal Advance Guard. D. Coy acting as Screen. Remainder of Battalion on Wagons.	O.H.7.
	5		Church Parade. 68 O.R Draft from Base.	O.H.7.
	6		Training continued. Divisional Advance Guard Scheme	O.H.7.
	7		Training continued. Individual training	O.H.7.
	8		Training continued. Individual training by A.N.C.Coys. C & D Co finished road practice.	O.H.7.
	9		Training continued. Individual training. A.C. finished road practice.	O.H.7.
	10		Training continued. Individual training. B & D. Coy. Jib firing.	O.H.7.
	11		Training continued. Divisional Tactical Exercise. Kind & trench attack.	O.H.7.
	12		Church Parade	O.H.7.
	13		Training continued. Individual training. D.C. & details Jibb firing.	O.H.7.
	14		Training continued. Individual training.	O.H.5.
	15		Training continued. Individual training	O.H.7.

W.W.Wood Lt Col

O.H.Y

SECRET
Army Form C. 2118.

WAR DIARY
INTELLIGENCE SUMMARY.
(Erase heading not required.)

AUGUST 1917.

2/5 Leicestershire Regt.

Instructions regarding War Diaries and Intelligence Summaries are contained in F. S. Regs., Part II. and the Staff Manual respectively. Title pages will be prepared in manuscript.

Place	Date	Hour	Summary of Events and Information	Remarks and references to Appendices
	1917. August			
BARASTRE	16		Training continued. Individual Training. Draft of 65 O.R. arrived from Base.	O.H.Y.
	17		Training continued. Individual Training.	O.H.Y.
	18		Training continued. Individual Training.	O.H.Y.
	19		Church Parade	J.A.D.
	20		Training continued. Individual Training. "A" Coy. inspected by Commanding Officer	O.H.Y.
	21		Training continued. Individual Training. B Coy. & D Coy. inspected by Commanding Officer. Next visited Dump inspected by Major-General Rowan Arrived party for SENLIS.	O.H.Y.
	22		The Brigade moved to the neighbourhood of SENLIS. A.& B. Coys. & Headquarters Coy. moved to a point 1 mile S.W. of LE SARS. C. & D. Coys. & Headquarters Company went into billets at first 1 mile S.W. of LE SARS, & moved thence to SENLIS, the rest of the Battalion being billeted further by motor buses. Hrs. of arrival at SENLIS. Battalion Headquarters on farm on RUE DEN.	O.H.Y. France 57D.
			HAUT.	
SENLIS (V.1.0.d)	23		Individual Training.	O.H.Y.
	24		Battalion Route March through HEDAUVILLE - WARLOY BAILLON - HENENCOURT - MILLENCOURT.	O.H.Y.
	25		Individual Training	O.H.Y.
	26		Rugby Services for 7th & 2/5 Leicestershire Regt., T. M. B., & 177 M.G.C.	O.H.Y.

Approved RED

Army Form C. 2118.
SECRET

2/5th Bn. The Leicestershire Regt.

WAR DIARY
or
INTELLIGENCE SUMMARY
(Erase heading not required.)

August 1917

Instructions regarding War Diaries and Intelligence Summaries are contained in F.S. Regs., Part II. and the Staff Manual respectively. Title pages will be prepared in manuscript.

Place	Date	Hour	Summary of Events and Information	Remarks and references to Appendices
SENLIS	Aug 1917 27		Battalion at Bath lby VARENNES — WARLOY BAILLON — HENENCOURT. Relieved by R.S.C.	AAF
	28		Practical Training. A.F.M. & N.C.O.'s Officers & N.C.O.s	AAF
	29		M.O. to see B.C. train. New Draft 24 hours.	AAF
	30		Attack practice continued. B.C. proceeds to ALBERT Station. Entrains to provide Transport.	AAF Strict 27mm [?] Regiment referenced 24.5
	31	5.21 p.m.	M.O. & party from ALBERT to [?] (on Cycles) from Rest Camp AMIENS & NAPLES. ST POL, HAZEBROUCK.	AAF 1/24,000

Original
Confidential
SECRET

Army Form C. 2118.

Instructions regarding War Diaries and Intelligence Summaries are contained in F. S. Regs., Part II. and the Staff Manual respectively. Title pages will be prepared in manuscript.

WAR DIARY or INTELLIGENCE SUMMARY.

(Erase heading not required.)

2/5 Lancashire Fus.

SEPTEMBER, 1917.

Place	Date	Hour	Summary of Events and Information	Remarks and references to Appendices
I.H.Q.	SEPT 1917 1		Map Reference – GRAVENSTAFEL Map Sheet Belgium 1 1/40,000 Sheet 28 N.W.2. Belgium 6A ST. JULIEN 28 N.E.1 " 6A ZONNEBEKE	
			Army reorganisation was completed. The Battn. now comprises four Coys. of 4 Platoons.	
			A, B, C, & D. Composed of MINNEZEELE Headquarters and H.Q. & A. & B. Coys.	
			Strength 37 Officers & 884 O.R. & 921 reinforcements 27 Officers & 816 O.R.	
MINNEZEELE	2		Church Parade	O/i/c
"	3		Training – Company attack practice	O/i/c
"	4		Route March Rue D'YPRES – HERZEELE – WORMHOUDT – KIEKENPUT J.15.c.76 – BRIEL.	O/i/c
"	5		Training – Battn. attack Practice	O/i/c
"	6		" – Individual Training – Battn. attack Practice	O/i/c
"	7		" – " – Coy " "	O/i/c
"	8		" – Route march	O/i/c
"	9		Church Parade – C.O. & 2nd in Command visited front line East of Ypres.	O/i/c
"	10		Training – Individual Training – 8 p.m. Coy attack Practice	O/i/c
"	11		" – Route march – School of Instruction Officers N.C.Os started.	O/i/c
"	12		" – Individual Training. 59th Div. Depot 13th draw (Capt Stoneham & 2/Lt. NORTHERN sent to rear)	O/i/c

Army Form C. 2118.

WAR DIARY
or
INTELLIGENCE SUMMARY.
(Erase heading not required.)

SEPTEMBER 1917

Instructions regarding War Diaries and Intelligence Summaries are contained in F.S. Regs., Part II. and the Staff Manual respectively. Title pages will be prepared in manuscript.

Place	Date 1917	Hour	Summary of Events and Information	Remarks and references to Appendices
WINNEZEELE	Sept. 13		Training — Batt". attack Practice	R.J.
"	14		" — Individual Training	R.J.
"	15		" — Brigade Tactical Exercise	R.J.
"	16		Church Parade	R.J.
"	17		Training — Individual Training	R.J.
"	18		" "	R.J.
"	19		" "	R.J.
"	20	2 a.m	Left WINNEZEELE by march Route for ESK Camp LG.B.24 arriving at 9 a.m	R.J.
ESK Camp	21	4.10	Training — Individual Training	
"	22		" "	
			R.S.M. Moslyn joined the Batt". & took over duties of R.M. attack of 2/Lt S.H. Wortham set. from 59th Div" on Sept 13th	
St. Jean	23	2 p.m	The Batt". marched into Reserve Trenches at St. Jean by train from CHADDERTON to YPRES and thence by Route March. Batt". Headquarters established at C.28.13 Hill 37, Hill 35, & ELMTREE CORNER formerly occupied	C.1
	24	7.30 p.m	The Batt". took over the front line trenches Hill 37, Hill 35, & ELMTREE CORNER from various units of the 176th Infan". Bde. Batt". H.Q. established at Bank Farm C.24.B.25.50	C.1

T2134. Wt. W708—776. 500000. 4/15. Sir J. C. & S.

Army Form C. 2118.

WAR DIARY or INTELLIGENCE SUMMARY.

(Erase heading not required.)

SEPTEMBER 1917

Instructions regarding War Diaries and Intelligence Summaries are contained in F.S. Regs., Part II. and the Staff Manual respectively. Title pages will be prepared in manuscript.

Place	Date	Hour	Summary of Events and Information	Remarks and references to Appendices
BANK FARM	25		The Battn occupied the trenches 2/4 & 2/5 Roughsedge killed	A.J.
ELM TREE CORNER	26	2 AM	Battn Headquarters established forward for the attack at ELM TREE CORNER D20 A05 60	A.J.
		3.50 AM	Bombardment started.	
		5.50 AM	Zero hour. The Battn went over to capture all enemy positions on HILL 37, Sheet 28 NE1 D20 A 45.50. A & B Coys in front line each 2 Platoons in front line, 1 Platoon in support. D Coy in support 2/4 R.A. Bourne killed Capt O.H. Beetham wounded 2Lt F.R. Farley wounded. Platoons kept within 100 yds of barrage in some cases though general tendency was to get too close to barrage. Hostile Arty fire caused little difficulty as leading waves well clone under barrage.	
		6.50 AM	All objectives taken Lt Col G.P. Wood wounded 2Lt Kerr Hutcheson wounded on both sides confirmed during day Battn Headquarters established in Pill Box on HILL 37 D20 A 65.85	
		4 pm	Enemy counter attack beaten back, Capt W.H. Elwes to	

T2134. Wt. W708-776. 500000. 4/15. Sir J.C. & S.

WAR DIARY
or
INTELLIGENCE SUMMARY.
(Erase heading not required.)

Army Form C. 2118.

SEPTEMBER 1917.

Place	Date	Hour	Summary of Events and Information	Remarks and references to Appendices
HILL 37	27		C.H.Q Hippus wounded. Lt Col. Gorman took command of the Battn. Bath. H.Q operators moved to Pill Box D20A7.8. Artillery very active on both sides during nght of Sept 26/27. Infantry on both sides very active during the day. Battn relieved part of 2/5th Lincolnshire Regt & part of the 2/5th Sherwood Foresters in the front line.	W.
"	28		Shelling not quite as heavy as previous days. Periods of comparative quiet. Back areas sh[elled] with HE & Gasshell at night. 2 Lt E Rose Gothen died of wounds. 2/Lt S.M.G Dallas wounded.	B+ A.T

T2134. Wt. W708-776. 500000. 4/15. Sir J. C. & S.

Army Form C. 2118.

WAR DIARY
or
INTELLIGENCE SUMMARY.
(Erase heading not required.)

SEPTEMBER 1917

Instructions regarding War Diaries and Intelligence Summaries are contained in F. S. Regs., Part II. and the Staff Manual respectively. Title pages will be prepared in manuscript.

Place	Date	Hour	Summary of Events and Information	Remarks and references to Appendices
	1917 Sept 29		Relieving Officers Anzac Brigade came up to view B.H.Q. Front line. B.H.Q. heavily shelled in consequence. Two direct hits on pill box. at night took over from line from 2/5th Bn. The Sherwood Foresters. Capt may ? Cpt Feilden shell of wounds to Coy 1/Canterbury Regt. Sent in support.	A.I
Old German Front Line	30		Day on the whole quiet B.H.Q. removed to new German Front line C 23 C 50.25 . 2.0. in rear no enemy aeroplanes dropped flares over Hill 37. Relieved by Otago Regiment at night - proceeded Call Reserve WIELTJE Road shelled on Road 25 casualties. Casualties Officers Killed 2/Lt C.Ranksey 2nd Lt R.A BOWIE Capt O H. FEILDEN 2/Lt L. ROBATHAN WOUNDED LtCol Q.P.G. WOOD A/CAPT H.W. OLIVER Lt C.H.G WYNNE 2nd Lt F.D. FARRELY 2nd LT S.W.G TALLIS. O.Ry Ranks Killed 61 wounded 184 Missing 25	A.S

Murray Lt Col
Commanding
2/S Lancashire Regt

9/5/17

CONFIDENTIAL ORIGINAL

Army Form C. 2118.

Instructions regarding War Diaries and Intelligence Summaries are contained in F.S. Regs., Part II. and the Staff Manual respectively. Title pages will be prepared in manuscript.

WAR DIARY of 2/5th Leicestershire / INTELLIGENCE SUMMARY
OCTOBER 1917

(Erase heading not required.)

Place	Date	Hour	Summary of Events and Information	Remarks and references to Appendices
VLAMERTINGHE	1917 Oct. 1		Strength 27 officers 613 other ranks = 640. Wk. sent in officers 49 & other ranks = 505.	Sheet - Belgium 28 N.W. 2.
			Boy guide found in Capt. Bevan at WIELTJE Road	
		7 p.m.	Marched to Huts/tents at VLAMERTINGHE. Total Casualties Officers killed 2. Died of wounds 2.	
			Wounded 5. Other ranks killed 54, Died of wounds 7, Wounded 184, Missing 25.	France Hazebrouck 5A
THIENNES	" 2	11 p.m.	Proceeded by train to THIENNES arriving at 6 p.m. Capt. H.G. BURDER rejoined unit from Training Base Depot at CALAIS.	
	" 3		Day spent in rest, cleaning up and equipping.	
	" 4	5-30 p.m.	Addressed by Major General. Training - individual training. Draft of 4 officers and 103 O.R. 2/25 H.WHETTON. T.MEAKIN B.W.SADLER and H.E.SCOFFIELD. Draft inspected by C.O.	
do.	" 5		Training - individual training. Thanksgiving Service. Draft inspected by C.O.	
do.	" 6	8 a.m.	Proceeded by March and bus route to BEAUMETZ-LEZ-AIRE arriving 1 p.m.	
BEAUMETZ-LEZ-AIRE	" 7	2-30 p.m.	Church Parade. Reinforcements 2/25 H.LEE. 2/25 J.H.KIRK 2/25 B.BLOXHAM. Whole Time in use.	
	" 8		Training - Individual training - Battn. bathed. CO and Adjutant attended conference at Bde. H.2.	
do.	" 9	10 a.m.	C.Os Inspection - Individual Training.	
do.	" 10	8-30 a.m.	Marched to CAMBLAIN-CHATELAIN arriving 3 p.m. CO. Intelligence officer & 2 Coy Commanders	

Army Form C. 2118.

WAR DIARY
or
INTELLIGENCE SUMMARY.
(Erase heading not required.)

Instructions regarding War Diaries and Intelligence Summaries are contained in F.S. Regs., Part II. and the Staff Manual respectively. Title pages will be prepared in manuscript.

Place	Date	Hour	Summary of Events and Information	Remarks and references to Appendices
BEAUMETZ-LEZ-AIRE	1917 Oct 10		Proceeded to trenches for tour of Battn. frontage.	
CAMBLAIN-CHATELAIN	11	11 am	Marched to HOUDAIN arriving 12-30 pm. 7 Officers proceeded for tour of the trenches.	
HOUDAIN	12	9 am	Marched to GOUY-SERVINS arrived 12 noon. Battn. H.Q. established at Q 35 c 8.8. Sheet 36B	
GOUY-SERVINS	13	9 am	Marched to TOTTENHAM CAMP arriving 2 pm. Battn. H.Q. established S 20 6 2.5. Sheet 36 C	
TOTTENHAM CAMP	"	5 pm	Proceeded to take over front line trenches from 10th Battn. (48th Royal Highlanders of Canada). Battn. H.Q. established at N 31 c. 6. 2. (France 36 c S.W.)	
OLD BREWERY	14		Everything quiet on our front. Casualties - 1 Killed, 2 wounded. Sanfricourd Lt. G.B. WILLIAMS. M.C. and 2/Lt COMINS.	
do	15		Quiet on our front. Occasional shelling on our Right. Relieving Officers from 178th Brigade and 2/4th Lincolnshire Regt. Come to Battn. H.Q. for tour of the front line.	
do	16	5 am	Shelling near Battn. H.Q. Company Commanders from 2/4th Lincs. Regt. arrived for tour of the front line. Casualties 1 O.R. wounded (S.I.W.) Captn. N.C. STONEHAM from 59th Div Depot Battn. Lt. + Q.M. E.H. THOMAS evacuated to England sick.	
do	17	10.30 pm	Battn. relieved by 2/4th Lincs Regt. Battn. moved into Support. Battn. H.Q. established at S 6 c. Piano dug out (Sheet France 36 c S.W.)	

Army Form C. 2118.

WAR DIARY
of
INTELLIGENCE SUMMARY.
(Erase heading not required.)

Instructions regarding War Diaries and Intelligence Summaries are contained in F. S. Regs., Part II. and the Staff Manual respectively. Title pages will be prepared in manuscript.

Place	Date	Hour	Summary of Events and Information	Remarks and references to Appendices
	1917 Oct			
PIANO DUG OUT	18	2.45pm	C.O. attended Conference at Battn Bde H.Q. Situation normal.	
do	19		Officers from Battn of Pickering Brigade came to H.Q. Reinforcement Officers 2/Lt F.S. HARRISON and 2/Lt W.S. BASS.	
do	20		Captured 2/8th Sherwood Foresters relieved Battn H.Q. as taking over from us.	
do	21	9pm	Relieved by 2/5th Sherwood Foresters. Battn H.Q. established at Alberta Camp X.18.a.70.70. Sheet 36 c. S.W.	
ALBERTA CAMP	22		Day spent in cleaning and equipping	
do	23		Individual training and working parties	
do	24		Individual training and working parties. Reinforcement of four officers 2/Lt D.T. SLOPER. 2/Lt T. CLARKSON 2/Lt P.A. GROOM and 2/Lt A.G. ESCUDIER	
do	25		Individual training and working parties. C.O. attended Conference at Brigade H.Q.	
do	26	2pm	Inspection of Transport by General MONTGOMERY. C.O. and Intelligence Officer visited 2/6th N. Staffs Bn H.Q. as taking over new Sector. A Coy Commanders went up the line to look round his Sector	
do	27		C.O attended Conference at Bde H.Q. Individual training and working parties. 7 Company officers went over new Sector.	

T2134. Wt. W708—776. 500000. 4/15. Sir J. C. & S.

Army Form C. 2118.

WAR DIARY
INTELLIGENCE SUMMARY.
(Erase heading not required.)

Place	Date	Hour	Summary of Events and Information	Remarks and references to Appendices
ALBERTA CAMP	1917 Oct 28	3 pm	Our General inspected Camp. British Aeroplane crashed opposite D Coy. H.Q.	
LIÉVIN	29	11 pm	Relieved 2/6th North Staffs Regt. in the line. Batln H.Q. established at M 23 d 20.80 (Map LENS 36 c. S.W. 1) Took over an American Officer 2/Lt MORRISON.	
do	30		Everything quiet on our front. No casualties. American officers attached to Brigade and our Batn. went up to the front line, one to A Coy and one to B Coy.	
do	31		Everything quiet on our front. No casualties. Gas projected in drums from our front at 6 pm. No retaliation. Our artillery shelled approaches east of LENS intermittently during the night with object of catching enemy troops relieving. Weather fine. Aeroplanes active.	

G. Munnnn? Lt Col
Commanding 2/5th Batt.
The Leicestershire Regt.

CONFIDENTIAL — ORIGINAL

Sheet 1

Army Form C. 2118.

WAR DIARY or INTELLIGENCE SUMMARY.
(Erase heading not required.)

2/5th Batt. The Lincolnshire Regt.

NOVEMBER

Instructions regarding War Diaries and Intelligence Summaries are contained in F.S. Regs., Part II. and the Staff Manual respectively. Title pages will be prepared in manuscript.

Place	Date	Hour	Summary of Events and Information	Remarks and references to Appendices
LIÉVIN	1917 Nov.1		Strength 41 officers 724 other ranks = 765. Will send 30 officers 569 other ranks = 599.	France LENS Sheet 36c SW1
		10.30a	American officers attached to 2 front line coys. left the line & returned to their HQrs	
		11.30am	C.O. attended conference at Bde HQrs. Ref Capt N.C. Shonham left Batt. for duty in England - authority W.O. letter No.121/Lincoln/837 A/13/8/17	Ref
"	2	9 a.m.	C.O. went round trenches with Brigadier & G.S.O.1 Inf. - 1 hr. enemy shelled vicinity of Batt. H.2 for ½ hour	
		6 p.m.	Gas drum projected from our front - no retaliation - Casualties 1 other rank wounded	
		11 p.m.	Inter-Company relief after 4 days in sector - 1 other rank wounded	
"	3	10 a.m.	Had General come to Batt. HQ. - C.O., Staff Capt. & A.D.M.S. inspected our site for R.A.P. near front line - visibility bad - aerial activity nil - all quiet on our front	
		9 p.m.	Small quantity of gas shells dropped between our support & reserve coys - 3 O.R. gassed	Ref
"	4		Quiet morning visibility fair - Support Coy shelled with Gas Shells. C.O. visited the 11th Manitoba on our left. Our artillery carried out barrages shoots from 6 p.m. until 6 a.m. - 2 O.R. killed 1 gassed	
"	5		Visibility fair - retaliation by our trench mortars for enemy trench mortar activity our right.	

Army Form C. 2118.

WAR DIARY
or
INTELLIGENCE SUMMARY.
(Erase heading not required.)

Sheet 2

Instructions regarding War Diaries and Intelligence Summaries are contained in F.S. Regs., Part II. and the Staff Manual respectively. Title pages will be prepared in manuscript.

NOVEMBER

France
Sheets 36b, 57c
57c 1/40,000

Place	Date	Hour	Summary of Events and Information	Remarks and references to Appendices
	1917			
LIÉVIN	Nov 5	12 mn	C Coy sent out patrol to locate enemy M.G. - no enemy discovered	B.J.
"	6	10 am	Visibility fair	B.J.
"		12 mn	Batt. relieved by 2/4th Lincolnshire Regt	
"	7		Batt. in support - men in cellars of village - Batt. supplying working parties all the time the Batt. was in support	B.J.
"	8	11.50	Visibility good - aerial activity - a few H.E. on main road near Coys billets	B.J.
"	9		do. H.E. shrapnel over our area at 3 min intervals from 9 am to 3 pm	R.J.
"	10	6/m	Gas drum projected from our front - no retaliation. Situation normal	J.J.
"	11	11 am	Boche aeroplane shot down by anti-aircraft gun in front of Batt. H.Q. 2/Lt O.C. Arnett joined the Batt. & Capt. T.C. Beasley struck off strength. Situation normal	S.J.
"	12			B.J.
"	13	7 pm	Batt. relieved by 4th Canadian Batt. Batt. moved party by Riencourt light Rly & march road to PETIT SERVINS arriving 3 am. - Capt Thomas C.F. transport taken on strength	
PETIT SERVINS	14		Day spent in cleaning & refitting	

Army Form C. 2118.

France
36 6/1, 57C, 57C
1/40,000

WAR DIARY
or
INTELLIGENCE SUMMARY.

(Erase heading not required.)

Sheet 3   NOVEMBER

Instructions regarding War Diaries and Intelligence
Summaries are contained in F.S. Regs., Part II.
and the Staff Manual respectively. Title pages
will be prepared in manuscript.

Place	Date	Hour	Summary of Events and Information	Remarks and references to Appendices
PETIT SERVINS	1917 Nov 15	9 a.m.	Training by Companies – C.O. inspected Coys. at work.	Ref
"	16	"	do	Ref
"	17	12.30 p.m.	Batt. moved by road route to HABARCQ arriving 5 p.m.	Ref
HABARCQ	18	11 a.m.	Church parade	Ref
"	19	4.30 p.m.	Batt. moved by road route via GOUY-EN-ARTOIS to BAILLEULVAL arriving 8.30 p.m. (7th Hd qrs)	Ref
BAILLEULVAL	20	10 a.m.	Batt. billeted	Ref
"	21	9 a.m.	Equipping & Special Training H.J.E. Kavn & 2/Lt G.H. Emersons struck off strength (sick)	Ref
"	"	11 a.m.	Batt. moved by road route via BERLES-AU-BOIS, BIENVILLERS-AU-BOIS, BUCQUOY to ACHIET-LE-PETIT, HENHAM CAMP SOUTH arriving 6 a.m.	
HENHAM CAMP SOUTH	22		Batt. rested – 4 Coy Commanders to Intelligence Office previous by bus to find area.	Ref
"	23	5 p.m.	Batt. left camp & entrained at ACHIET-LE-GRAND at 10 p.m. for FINS arriving 1 a.m. + Marched to DESSART WOOD Batt. formed up & Coys. Res. for CAMBRAI battle	Ref
DESSART WOOD	24	10 a.m.	C.O. + Coy Commdrs went up to reconnoitre new line & approaches Hind:	Ref
"	25	"	2nd in command, Adjutant & 2/Lts in command of Coys. proceeded to reconnoitre line between MARCOING and MASNIERES	Ref
"	26	9 a.m.	Training by Companies	Ref

SHEET 4

WAR DIARY
or
INTELLIGENCE SUMMARY.
(Erase heading not required.)

Army Form C. 2118.

France
57c 1/50000

Place	Date	Hour	Summary of Events and Information	Remarks and references to Appendices
	1917			
DESSART WOOD	Nov 27	2.30 pm	Batt. moved by road north to TRESCAULT arriving 4 pm – Company commanders went with Brigadier to reconnoitre forward area	O.C.
TRESCAULT	" 28	2.30 pm	Batt. marched to FLESQUIRES via RIBECOURT (B'de in Support)	
FLESQUIRES	" 29		Batt. garrison in dugouts – visibility good – aerial activity	
	30	11 am	Activity all day on front – 4 Bosche 'planes shot down in our area + 1 enemy + 1 R.F.C. observation balloon shot down – 2 O.R. wounded	
		5.30 pm	Batt. moved forward + occupied HINDENBURG SUPPORT LINE just outside village. Occasional shelling by H.A. during night	O.C.

EG Wineur Lt Col
Commanding 2/5 Bn. The Lincolnshire Regt

CONFIDENTIAL

ORIGINAL

Army Form C. 2118.

Instructions regarding War Diaries and Intelligence Summaries are contained in F. S. Regs., Part II. and the Staff Manual respectively. Title pages will be prepared in manuscript.

WAR DIARY or INTELLIGENCE SUMMARY.
(Erase heading not required.)

2/5th Leicestershire Regt.

Ref. Sheets 57c & 57b

Vol 11

Place	Date	Hour	Summary of Events and Information	Remarks and references to Appendices
FLESQUIRES	DEC 1	11 a.m.	Activity along the whole front — visibility good. C.O. attended Conference at Brigade. 2 Coys moved up to rear support. Battn through 37 Off, 719 O.R.s 1 with and 30 Off, 580 R. in support Batt. M.2	A.J.
"	2	5 p.m.	Battn relieved 2/5th So. Staffs on right front line — 3 Coys in front, 1 in support. Established at CANTAING MILL. Map 57c E 26 d 74	A.J.
CANTAING MILL	3		Visibility good. General activity normal.	A.J.
"	4	4 a.m.	Selection normal. Battn H.Q. established on German dugout under Battn toff. 37 Off, 679 O.R. dugout 57c K 7 B 79 dugout - 1 2 O.R. Wounded	A.J.
FLESQUIRES CHURCH	5		Situation quiet. Lt Col H.B. Toffy of 2/5th Lincs arrived at our H.2 to be advanced Brigade Commander. Major G.I.S. Wenart to Hospital (sick)	A.J.
OLD Bde. HQ.	6	1 p.m.	Battn H.2 moved to Old Puggest H.2 R24 b M.8	A.J.
FLESQUIRES		3 p.m.	Enemy attacks in large numbers. 59th Div Oxford line under attack with strong withdrawn. Enemy arts when our line I known required with Flesqu. Viens 1 German machine gun (Reg N) captured by N.10 platoon. 3 prisoners brought into Battn H.2 by 2/4 Lincs. Our casualties. 1 officer wounded 17 O.R. killed, 25 O.R. wounded and Lt Col C Mauger (Com) & Capt F W. Goff, 2 prisoners brought to Hospital (sick)	A.J.
"	7		Hery shelling by 2/4th Lincs. Lt Col G Grimman sent to Hospital (sick) tak command by Capt. F. W. Goff. Battn H.2 by 2/7 Sherwoods	A.J.
"	8		Enemy activity increased on our side & many men heavy streets. Information obtained from a prisoner 2/5 c Evans to Hospital (sick) 7/17/17	A.J.
"	9	2 pm	Any activity. Reserve brought in by 2/5th Lincs	A.J.
			Battn relieved by 2/5 Sherwoods	
TRESCAULT	10	12 noon	Battn assembled in old German trench before TRESCAULT. Battn & map 57c 94c54 moved by 2/5th Leic. Regt. & proceeded to camp at LECHELLE, arriving 4 p.m.	A.J.

Battn H.Q. 2/5th Leic. Regt. P.25 6.00

Army Form C. 2118.

WAR DIARY
or
INTELLIGENCE SUMMARY.
(Erase heading not required.)

Ref. Reel 57c
 " 57e

Place	Date	Hour	Summary of Events and Information	Remarks and references to Appendices
LECHELLE	11		Day spent in equipping Battery. Total casualties for tour in line 2 offr. 57 ORs. Training by Capt. Major J.R.B. Vincent struck off strength.	(5 killed) A/f
"	12	9 a.m.		A/f
"	13	9 a.m.	—	A/f
"	14	11.55 a.m.	Batty. moved to TRESCAULT into new billets 2/Lts. Hue, Pigott, Battn & B. Worthy. 5yc & 4 yety. Heavy shelling by 5.9 Battery.	A/f A/f
TRESCAULT	15	9 a.m.		A/f
"	16	2 p.m.	Transport lines moved from NEUVILLE to BERTINCOURT. Batt. supplying working parties.	A/f
"	17	5 p.m.	Batty. relieved 2/8 Staffords in HINDENBURG SUPPORT (RIGHT) Bn in H.Q. Res. 57c R 24 on 84. Working parties. Hostile artillery fire on both sides.	A/f A/f
HINDENBURG SUPPORT	18		do	A/f
"	19		do	B/f
"	20		do	A/f
"	21			B/f
"	22	6 p.m.	10 OR killed 2 wounded. Battn. relieved by 12 K. Battn. Manchester Regt. & proceeded to line vacated by relieving Battn. at BUTLERS CROSS Q3.6 & 2 (Sheet 57c).	B/f
BUTLERS CROSS	23	10.30 a.m.	Battn. relieved by 10 Battn. W. Ridg. & moved by march route to ROCQUIGNY arriving 2 p.m. Capt. R.K. Moir rejoined Battn. & assumed command from 2/Lt. Day spent in equipping & cleaning up.	B/f
ROCQUIGNY	24	10.4 a.m.		B/f
"	25	5.30 a.m.	Battn. marched to BAPAUME & entrained at 10 a.m. for TINQUES. Corr. bus party. March to start being at PENIN arriving 3 p.m.	B/f
PENIN	26	9 a.m.	Battn. resting. Heavy fall of snow.	B/f
"	27	10 a.m.	Kit inspection by C.O. Battn. celebrated Xmas. Lt. Col. F.W. Bullock Marsh & Lt. & Paston & Mountra'. commanded from this date.	B/f

Army Form C. 2118.

Ref: Sheet 57C
51

WAR DIARY
or
INTELLIGENCE SUMMARY.
(Erase heading not required.)

Instructions regarding War Diaries and Intelligence Summaries are contained in F. S. Regs., Part II. and the Staff Manual respectively. Title pages will be prepared in manuscript.

Place	Date	Hour	Summary of Events and Information	Remarks and references to Appendices
PENIN	28	8.45	Training by Coys. C.O. & Adjt attended a tactical scheme for 177 Inf Bde.	
	29	8.45	2/Lt Hilger proceeded to join R.F.C. Training by Coys.	
	30	7.30	Church Parade. C.O. 2/5 Lon. Command & Adjutant attending conference at Brigade.	
		2/5	Draft of 138 O.Rs. arrived.	
	31	8.45	Training by Coys. Brigade inspection billets.	

J. W. Riddle
Lt. Col.
Commanding 2/5th Batln. The London Regt.

Army Form C. 2118.

2/6 Bn. Leicestershire Regt.

SECRET
WAR DIARY
INTELLIGENCE SUMMARY.
(Erase heading not required.)

Instructions regarding War Diaries and Intelligence Summaries are contained in F. S. Regs., Part II. and the Staff Manual respectively. Title pages will be prepared in manuscript.

Place	Date	Hour	Summary of Events and Information	Remarks and references to Appendices
PENIN C.22.d.1.4. Sheet 51c. France.			JANUARY. 1918.	
	1	8.45 am	Battalion School started. Coy training in defence & counter attack & firing on range. 36 Officers and 685 O.R.	A.L
	2	8.45 am	Battalion Advance Guard Scheme & firing on the range. Lecture by Divisional two Officer to all W.O.s. N.C.O.s.	R.L
		2.15 pm	Reinforcements 8 O.R. arrived.	
	3	8.45 am	Battalion School & Company Training & firing on range.	R.L
		9.30 am	The C.O., 2nd in Command, Adjutant, all Company Commanders and Platoon Officers with exception of 1 per company attended 177 Infantry Brigade Tactical Exercise.	
	4	11.45 am	Company Training. The Battalion in defence and counter attack. Battalion Rallying by bugle in afternoon. 6 O.R. Reinforcements arrived.	A.L
	5	8.45 am	Company Training and firing of short Musketry Course. Lewis Gunners firing Revolver Course. 2/Lieut. F.J. Harrison evacuated to England sick.	R.L
		9.30 am	C.O., 2nd in Command, and Adjutant attended 177 Infantry Brigade Tactical Exercise.	
	6	11.15 am	Battalion - C. of E. Service.	R.L
	7	8.45 am	All indifferent shots firing on range. Coy training in Battalion in attack deploying from Attack. R.A.M.C. class for junior N.C.O.s and privates likely to become N.C.O.s daily at 9.0 am.	R.L
	8	8.45 am	Company Training & firing on range. All rifles inspected by Brigade Armourer Sergeant.	A.L

(X7092) Wt. W12930/M1293 75 10 6. 1/17. D. D. & L. Ltd. Forms/C.2118/14.

SECRET

WAR DIARY
or
INTELLIGENCE SUMMARY.

(Erase heading not required.)

Army Form C. 2118.

Place	Date	Hour	Summary of Events and Information	Remarks and references to Appendices
PENIN	9	8.45 am	Company Training - Tactical Exercises. Lewis Gunners firing a revolver course.	
		9.30 am	C.O. 2nd in Command - Adjutant. All Company Commanders & Platoon Commanders with the exception of 1 per Coy. attended 177 Inf. Bde. Tactical Exercise.	
	10	8.45 am	Battn. Drill. All Lewis Gunners firing on range. Battalion bathed by Coys.	
	11	11.45 am	Battalion Tactical Exercise - Advance Guard.	
		9.50 am	Battalion inspected by C.O.	
	12	8.45 am	Company Training. Companies firing rapid fire competition.	
	13	11.0 am	Battalion and Detachments C of E Service in the village. Major General Commanding 59th Division presented medals and ribbons to officers and other ranks.	
	14	8.45 am	Company Training. Transport firing on range. Capt. F.H. Gaff resumes the duties of 2nd in Command as from 12th inst. 2/Lieut B.W. Sadler retaken on the strength and 37 O.R's. arrived.	
	15	8.45 am	Coy Training & Battalion Tactical Scheme - Outposts. 7 Reinforcements (Officers) arrived:- 2/Lieut F.H. Gardner, 2/Lieut L. Blackham, 2/Lieut W. Priestley, 2/Lieut R.S. Shoban, 2/Lieut H. Cocell, 2/Lt. F. Clark. 2.30 pm. Battalion Pack Run.	
	16		Training by Companies.	
	17	8.45 am	Coy Training & firing on range for indifferent shots. Battalion bathed by Coys.	
		10.30 am	Lecture by 3rd Army Instructor firing Battery at HIGNEREUL (F21.B central) 2nd in Command & Battn Q.M. Sgt. & books.	
		9.30 am	C.O. 2nd in Command, Adjutant. All O.C. Coys & Platoon Commanders with exception of 1 per Coy attended 177 Inf. Bde Tactical Scheme.	

WAR DIARY or INTELLIGENCE SUMMARY.

Army Form C. 2118.

Place	Date	Hour	Summary of Events and Information	Remarks and references to Appendices
PENIN	17	8.45 am	Tactical Exercise – The deployments of a Battn for Attack and the Battn in attack.	A.J
	18	2.30	Tactical Exercise for Officers and N.C.O's.	A.J
	19	10 am	Battalion running in Inf Bde long distance run. Lt. Col. T.W. Rublick left to command 1st Dorset Regt.	A.J
	20	11 am	Brigade C. of E. Service at AMBRINES 1.8.6.1. Major D.L. Brereton. i/c of Arrangements.	A.J
	21	8.45	Company training – firing on range. Advance party of Capt N.W. Olsen and 26 O.Rs proceeded to Third Army Clearing Depot, ACHIET-LE-GRAND, Sheet 57c. 5.10 central.	B.J P.J
	22	8.45	Company Training. Main party of 2/Lt F.H. Gardner, 2/Lt W.W. Weall and 144 O.Rs proceeded to Third Army Clearing Depot, ACHIET-LE-GRAND.	P.J B.J
	23	9.30	C.O., 2nd in Command, Adjutant & all Coy Cmdrs & Platoon Commanders with the exception of 1 per Coy for Training attended 177 Infantry Brigade Tactical Exercise. 10 O.Rs. reinforcements arrived.	A.J
	24	8.45	Coy Training and firing. Lewis Gunners firing on range.	A.J
	25	8.45	Coy Training & firing. C.O. & 2 i/c in Command attended Tactical Exercise of 176 Infantry Brigade on rangefires.	O.J
	26	8.45	Individual Training.	O.J
	27	9.30	C. of E. Parade.	B.J
	28	9.30	Demobilising Battn. 2/Lt J.H. Kirk proceeded to Base on special duty.	B.J
	29	9.0	C.O. inspected draft of Officers & men for various units of Leicestershire Regt. on Battn Parade Gds. Capt. Hickson & 14 O.Rs returned from III Army Clearing Depot.	A.J

SECRET.
WAR DIARY
or
INTELLIGENCE SUMMARY.

Army Form C. 2118.

(Erase heading not required.)

Place	Date	Hour	Summary of Events and Information	Remarks and references to Appendices
PENIN	30		2 officers 50 O.R's. posted to 1st Bn. Leicestershire Regt. 2 officers and 42 O.R's proceeded to join, 9 officers & 196 O.R's posted and 5 officers and 158 O.R.s proceeded to join 1/4th Leicestershire Regt. 6 officers and 201 O.R.s posted and 7 officers & 162 O.R.s proceeded to join 1/5th Bn. Leicestershire Regt. 12 officers and 207 O.R's posted and 9 officers & 168 O.R's proceeded to join 1/1st Bn. Leicestershire Regt.	R.
	31		7 officers and 171 O.R.s posted & 1 officer and 81 O.R.s proceeded to join 2/4th Battn. Leicestershire Regt.	R.J.
LIGNEREUIL	1.2.1918.	2.pm	Battn. H.Q. marched to C.22.c.28 (Map 51/C.) Major D.L Brereton left to join 2nd B. De.1. Major G.H.Gill took over command	

Cmdg. 2/5th Bn. Leicestershire Regt

Major.

www.ingramcontent.com/pod-product-compliance
Lightning Source LLC
Chambersburg PA
CBHW081457160426
43193CB00013B/2514